LEARN
CURRENCIES

Name _____

AUD is for
Australian Dollar

AUD aud

LEARN CURRENCIES

Name _____

BTC

is for Cryptocurrency

BTC btc

LEARN CURRENCIES

C$

CAD is for
Canadian Dollar

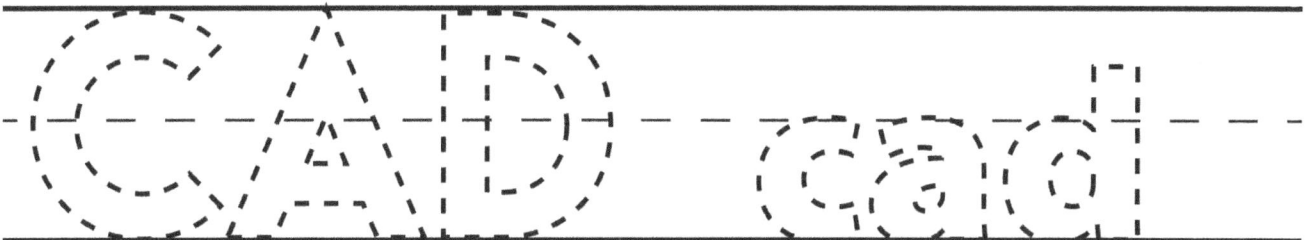

CAD cad

7

LEARN
CURRENCIES

F

CHF is for
Swiss Franc

CHF chf

LEARN
CURRENCIES

Name _____

EUR is for European Union

EUR   eur

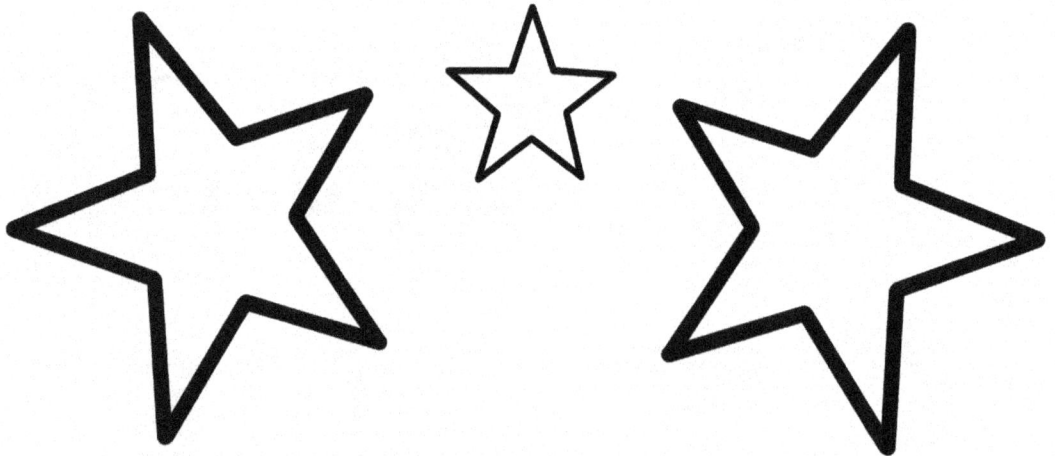

LEARN CURRENCIES

Name _____

GBP **is for British Pound**

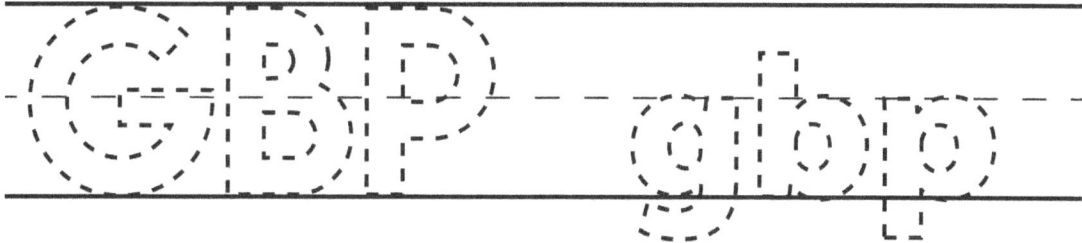

13

LEARN
CURRENCIES

Name _____

JPY **is for Japanese Yen**

JPY   jpy

LEARN
CURRENCIES

Name _____

NZ$

NZD is for New Zealand Dollar

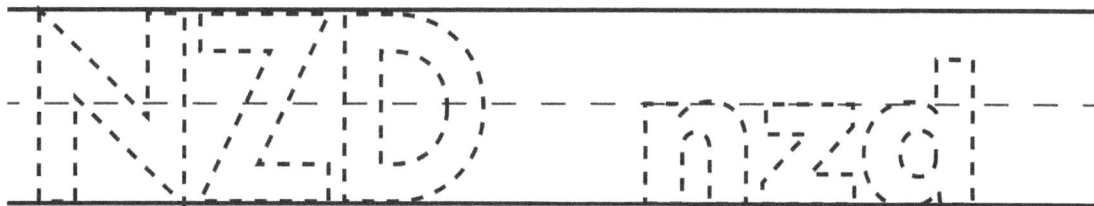

NZD   nzd

LEARN
CURRENCIES

Name _____

USD **is for American Dollar**

USD usd

19

LEARN
CURRENCIES

Name _____

XAU

XAU is for Gold

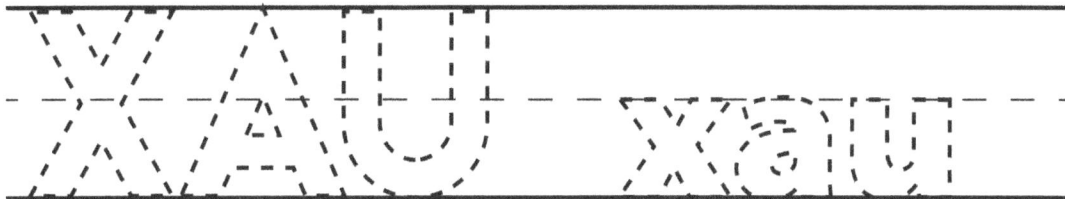

XAU   xau

Practice what you learned:

Congratulations!!

_____

Name

ISBN: 978-1-7361206-0-6